I *am* ME

DISCOVER THE
LIFE PATH COLOUR IN YOU!

AMANDA J HOFFMANN
MARK WENTWORTH

Cover & Illustrations: Amanda J Hoffmann

First Edition 2024

ISBN: 987-1-0687638-1-6

Published by The Colour House (UK)

"A brilliant, easy to follow, introduction to the world of Life Path Colours, offering ways we can use colour to connect with our innate being and purpose"

Sahar Milani - Brand Specialist & Podcast Host

I Am ME - "describes the essence and the depth of the wisdom behind the colour path ... revealing how every colour carefully selects, nurtures, and transforms into life companions ... steering the soul towards its blossoming into a higher existence."

Sonia Lakhiani - Art of Living Foundation

"I found this book an easy read and simple to grasp, while still coming away with new insights, practical wisdom and enjoyable exercises to play with."

Andrew Barrett - AI Web Developer & Entrepreneur

"What a wonderfully beautiful, simple, clear guide to the magical world of colour and how it heals so many aspects of our being. Thank you!!"

Denise Hadden - Light Field Therapist

This book is dedicated to you, The Reader.
And to the Life Path Colours within us all.

CONTENTS

OUR COLOUR JOURNEYS

Having been a teacher, I have always worked with words, been a communicator and someone who shared my ideas. Since putting this profession behind me, I have moved on to other ways to communicate and connect.

My own Life Path Colour story is quite directly connected with both Mark and with writing this book. Discovering that my colour is Blue - The Storyteller - has confirmed what I have probably known in my heart but have suppressed for the longest time. There is clarity in understanding this authentic self. There is wisdom in knowing how it affects me in life as I move through it. While I was working through each of the Life Path Colours and learning about them, I then came to write up the description of my colour Blue and there was an OMG moment or two. Each and every item rang so very true to me. What a lesson in self-awareness!

I have known Mark for a number of years, being familiar with his work in the world of colour and also the wide range of his expertise. I've worked with him previously in my role as a journal editor and I have also attended his programs online. In November 2023, Mark was running a workshop in my home city of Adelaide, Australia, and we met again in person.

It was after his full day session of Life Path Colour exploration, that I wrote a short piece called 'I am Me, I am BLUE'. A little later, the idea formed of a book on the subject. I wanted to create a book introducing the idea of Life Path Colours in a simple way; to offer people who may not be familiar with the concept, a starting point to discover the potential of colour.

So, here it is, a little book about Life Path Colours.
I hope it adds meaning to your life - and some colour, too.

Amanda

When I first discovered my Life Path Colour nearly forty-years ago I had quite mixed emotions. On one hand it was a relief, for here was a colour system that was assigning me a Gold colour to help me make sense of my thoughts and feelings and way of seeing the world. On the other hand, the full description of this colour felt way beyond who I thought I was or ever could be. Yet over the years I have grown into Gold, becoming and living the very things I just didn't think were possible for me back then.

I remember the first time I gave a talk about Life Path Colours, this was quite a feat in itself. When I was younger I was painfully shy. The idea of speaking in front of people was a terrifying thought and one I tried my best to avoid. And yet, here I was not ten years later about to give a talk in a public space to a group of strangers. Even if I wasn't aware of it then, my Gold Path knew the way.

My original intention for that talk back then, and continues to be now, is to help people become more conscious of this amazing thing called Life Path Colours.

When Amanda shared her ideas for this book I was excited, and without hesitation said Yes! Why? Because a Gold Sage, who can easily wax lyrical and poetically about Life Path Colours until the cows come home, needs the collaboration and support of a Blue Storyteller. One who reminds him, quite often I might add, to keep it simple!

And that's exactly it. Colour is simple. In its simplicity, your Life Path Colour will - if you allow it to - guide and support you to reveal, to become and to live, a contented, fulfilled and wholehearted life. And honestly, you can't get any better than that. It's not just any life, but YOUR life. The one you were born to live.

Mark

WELCOME ...

Colour simply is. It adorns every part of our existence. It gives meaning to our day to day lives. It brings the inanimate aspects of the world to life in a way that only the Soul can understand. Where there is colour, there is life.

This subject is as far-reaching and unending as the Universe itself. It's as shallow as the lapping waves on a white sandy beach, and at the same time as deep as the Mariana Trench.

Have you ever thought that as well as colour being a choice, it's also true that colour chooses you? That sliver of visible light that makes up the electro-magnetic spectrum has its own power. And the influence of colour is enough to last a lifetime. It will choose which part of its wisdom it wants you to explore, and which aspects to reveal to the world.

In this book, we share with you what might be called the more 'invisible' side to the colours we can see. These 'inner' colours are the Life Paths Colours. They are the colours which reside in each one of us, within the depths of the Soul.

These colours act as guides when we become lost. They act as companions when we're called to follow an unknown path. They act as reminders that we never walk this path alone.

Join us as we step across the threshold into this wonderful world of colour. The colours are waiting to meet you.

Red has been pacing impatiently, waiting for you to arrive. Yellow has been questioning why you haven't started yet, and Indigo has been quietly observing and sensing your exact arrival. And Gold is inviting you to follow a new, yet familiar path. Your own Life Path.

So, let the Colour Journey begin!

'COLOUR IS THE PLACE
WHERE OUR MIND
AND THE UNIVERSE MEET'

PAUL KLEE

STOP AND LOOK AROUND . . . WHAT DO YOU SEE?

You might see people doing various things. You will see different scenes and settings. Physical objects and the natural world. What's the one common thing between all of them?

It's something so very visible that it's somewhat invisible. It's the one constant that we are surrounded by from the moment we are born until the day we leave this world. It's colour!

Colour is simply light made visible. The colours we see are around us even if we're not always aware of them. There are colours that attract and call to us. Colours that tell us when to stop and pay attention. Colours that ask us to rest and relax.

In countries with distinct seasons, Nature shows us clearly which season we are in. Each one having its own shade and tone. On any day, we choose the colours to wear. We want to express our mood and how we are feeling. The colours we choose for our homes are more than decor. These colours nourish and support us when we return home after being outside in the world.

Colour in this subtle form acts, in a way, as a communicator and a signpost for those around us. They tell everyone that "This is who I am. I am Me through the colours I choose."

While colour choices express who we are in our daily life, what if there was a colour that comes from the inside? A colour with the potential to guide and support us in becoming more fully who we were born to be.

Just as a rose can never be anything but a rose, and an acorn can only become an oak tree, neither the rose nor the acorn 'try' to be what they are. They simply grow into their original and unique way of being. They grow into their potential.

WHAT IF … ?

What if you knew beyond doubt that *who you are* is totally and fully enough? What if *being you* meant you didn't have to *try to be you* but could simply 'be'?

And just like the acorn becoming an oak tree, what if you were able to grow into your own original, beautiful, and uniquely perfect way of being? Imagine how you might behave if this were true. Imagine how you might feel.

Discovering and knowing your Life Path Colour could be described as being given a road map. It gives you a way of experiencing the world in your very own way. Seeing life from your individual colour perspective can help you make sense of the 'How' and Why' of feeling and behaving the way you do. Helping you to respond instead of reacting in the world.

Having this understanding is also a way of communicating and knowing the other colours, as a way to foster deeper connection and stronger relationships with those around you. And this is all possible through the language of this amazing system called Life Path Colours.

Discovering and nurturing your Life Path Colour is about being authentic and true *to yourself* and *your purpose*. Why try to follow the Red path when you were born to be on the Violet one? Why be anything other than who you were meant to be and who Nature intended you to be?

Learning the language of Life Path Colours gives you the potential for greater self-awareness and the possibility for change. And to follow the path that is destined for YOU!

I AM ME. I AM ON MY OWN LIFE PATH.

WHAT ARE LIFE PATH COLOURS?

In ancient times, people looked to the stars for guidance. They looked to their gods and goddesses as well. Today, we might consider star signs and consult astrological charts. We might look to psychological or personality frameworks to help us understand who we are and why we behave as we do.

And numbers? They once played a part in the everyday life of the ancients, who developed their own systems. In many religions, numbers had a mystical meaning. The philosopher and mathematician, Pythagoras understood the deeper meaning of numbers and this Life Path Colour system follows the principles of numerology that Pythagorus developed.

From birth, our life journey is defined by significant events. The first day of school, leaving home, our first job. Let's not forget our first love! We often imagine these key life events on a timeline, or as markers on a pathway through life.

A Life Path Colour journey is much the same. There are nine Life Path Colours and one of them will be yours.

Your Life Path Colour is derived from your date of birth. This might seem like a random day with no special meaning. But in many Ancient, Eastern and Indigenous belief systems, it is thought that a Soul chooses the day and exact time, family and location, as well as the period in history to be born. This is in order for the Soul to fulfil its greatest potential.

A Life Path Colour could be described as the foundation on which we stand, and a path to exploring our different "ways to be". Each Life Path Colour presented here is also symbolised by an archetype which offers us guidance and understanding of our basic core behaviours.

CALCULATE YOUR LIFE PATH COLOUR

To calculate your Life Path Colour, take your date of birth and add all the numbers together. Keep adding them together until it is reduced to a single digit between 1 – 9.

For example: 28 . 10 . 1992

2 + 8 + 1 + 0 + 1 + 9 + 9 + 2 = 32. 3 + 2 = 5.

Number 5 is Blue

SO ... WHAT COLOUR ARE YOU?

1 - RED

2 - ORANGE

3 - YELLOW

4 - GREEN

5 - BLUE

6 - INDIGO

7 - VIOLET

8 - ROSE

9 - GOLD

MY LIFE PATH COLOUR IS ....

I AM ME. I AM ....

DISCOVER WHAT IT MEANS TO BE YOU

This book is an introduction to the potential of Life Path Colours as a guide and an inspiration. It is an entry point, rather than a complete or final destination for this journey.

The following pages give descriptions and details of each Life Path Colour. There are explanations of key traits for each one. For all of the nine Life Path Colours, there is an Archetype, key descriptors and an overview of the colour personality.

There will be things that make sense to you right away. You might think, "Yes, absolutely. This is really me." There may be other things you might not agree with. Things that you don't see or recognise in yourself.

If this is true for you, why not show your Life Path Colour story to your family and friends? It may be that they see things in you that you don't immediately recognise in yourself.

What if you don't actually 'like' your colour? What if you don't like being a Red, or a Green or a Blue?

Firstly - and importantly - it doesn't mean that you have to wear your Life Path Colour. Unless you want to, that is.

Sometimes the qualities of your Life Path Colour can seem very different from your lived experience of the colour itself.

In fact, over the years, we have found that Life Path Colours invite us to rethink our relationship and thoughts about colours per se. You might ask yourself what the colour may be trying to tell you. Our individual colour will have a lot to say to us, if we are but open to listen.

So, don't worry if you don't 'like' your Life Path Colour. This is really more about *being it and living it.*

'MERE COLOUR ...

CAN SPEAK TO THE SOUL IN

A THOUSAND DIFFERENT WAYS'

OSCAR WILDE

THE LIFE PATH NUMBER

ONE

IS LIFE PATH COLOUR

RED

I *am* ME. I *am* RED

"I am the REBEL"

I am …
    Active.
    Dynamic.
    Spontaneous.

RED people are the
pioneers of the spectrum.
Number 1 in all they do!

IF YOUR LIFE PATH COLOUR IS RED

Dear RED, being you is all about being bold and brave. Being brave doesn't have to be a big thing. It is whatever it means to you. A small change in your life can be your 'brave step'.

You are the Rebel pioneer of the spectrum. When other people say, "You can't" - your reply is, "Yes, I can". Hearing "No" only gives you more determination to make it happen.

If your Life Path Colour is RED, you are active and dynamic. Always on the go, you live an excitement-filled life. You want to experience everything, just for the sake of it. And patience? It's not the first word in your vocabulary!

In work life, you could definitely be your own boss. If this is not your situation, then you will prefer an easy-going boss because you are probably the one taking the lead anyway.

You are someone who speaks their mind and says exactly what they feel. Will you often shock people? Perhaps. But this can sometimes be the price of being so honest.

Following a RED Life Path, you might be seen wearing bold, daring, statement clothing. This is an expression of your strong and vibrant personality.

Your health? Remember to take time to relax and recharge your battery. If not, you may burn out, leading to frustration that you aren't able to do everything you love to do.

Emotionally, you feel it all. From being in and out of love, sad, hurt, or angry. You don't talk about how you felt yesterday. You live in the 'now'!

People on a RED Life Path know what they want, surrounding themselves with similarly outgoing and energetic people.

Colour Your World RED

Choose a RED word that resonates.
Use it in this AFFIRMATION

"I am ...."

THE LIFE PATH NUMBER

TWO

IS LIFE PATH COLOUR

ORANGE

I *am* ME. I *am* ORANGE

"I am the JESTER"

I am …
Fun-Loving.
Popular.
Patient.

ORANGE people are the spectrum's carefree ones. They live a balanced life!

IF YOUR LIFE PATH COLOUR IS ORANGE

Dear ORANGE, you remind us that we all deserve to be happy and enjoy life to the full. Others may take life too seriously while you are looking for the pleasures of life. If you are accused of being too easy-going, your reply is, "Yes life can be difficult but it's better to see the good and what we do have, rather than only see what is lacking or missing.

If your Life Path Colour is ORANGE, you live a cheerful and balanced life. Your fun-loving energy makes you a joy to be around. You are a very popular person at any social event!

An important part of your life is food, which may be a hobby, or could just as easily be a career. But be aware that food could become an emotional prop, in one way or another.

You have the gift of seeing both sides of a situation. This makes you a good mediator because your aim is to help facilitate an outcome which benefits everyone. When people ask for your opinion, you will find positives in different views. Perhaps you are often called on to provide counselling or support. But be careful not to take on the burden of other people's problems. Learn to say "No" without feeling guilty.

Do you notice your emotions ebb and flow, especially around the full moon? Orange relates to the water element so check whether your emotions follow the moon cycle. If this is the case, you can make plans for the best times to do certain tasks. Helping to maintain balance of emotions is the goal.

You are a truly social soul. Being with friends and sharing a meal and good times together is your happy place.

People on an ORANGE Life Path are playful and happy. A life full of pleasure and adventure awaits!

Colour Your World ORANGE

Choose an ORANGE word that resonates.
Use it in this AFFIRMATION

"I am ...."

THE LIFE PATH NUMBER

THREE

IS LIFE PATH COLOUR

YELLOW

I *am* ME. I *am* YELLOW

"I am the WARRIOR"

I am …
Cheerful.
Hopeful.
Analytical.

YELLOW people are the optimists of the spectrum. They lead a stimulating life!

IF YOUR LIFE PATH COLOUR IS YELLOW

Dear YELLOW, you are like a ray of sunshine and a welcome presence in any room. You radiate the energy of hope and optimism especially at times when it may be lacking in others.

You have an ability to cut through high emotion and get straight to the point. You make clear what needs to be done in the moment. You are the one with focused attention, always seeking the answer to why something is so.

You love to socialise, and people love to hear your stories. Your quick wit and mercurial way of thinking has a way of spicing them up. Can we say, adding colour to the narrative?

You have a fine intellect and are often surrounded by books on a wide range of topics. And woe betide the person who dare suggest that maybe you have too many books on the bedside table, in the sitting room, the kitchen ...

If your Life Path is YELLOW, you need to be interested in things - people, too - otherwise you tend to become easily bored. This can be very obvious to others if you don't watch what you say or give away feelings in your facial expressions!

You have an eye for detail and an analytical mind. This can cross into your emotional life because you place everything and everyone into their own little box. This includes emotions. For you, there has to be logic to everything, even feelings.

Your health? Mental stress and anxiety can manifest in the stomach and insomnia. So, try not to overdo caffeine and sugar. These stimulate the mind, and yours is active enough!

People on a YELLOW Life Path are stimulating and joyous people to be around.

Colour Your World YELLOW

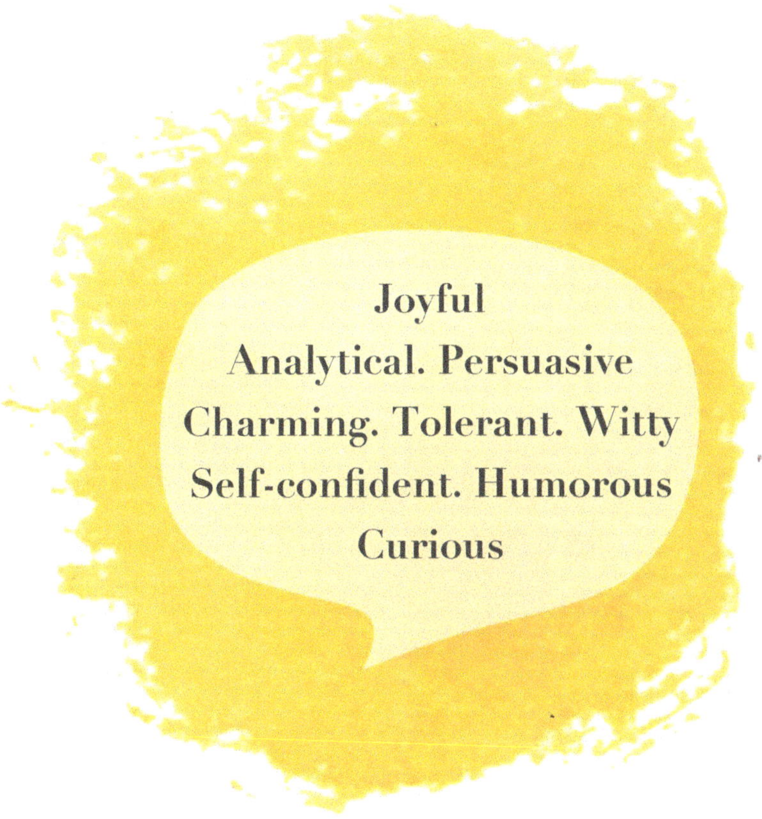

Choose a YELLOW word that resonates.
Use it in this AFFIRMATION

"I am ...."

THE LIFE PATH NUMBER

FOUR

IS LIFE PATH COLOUR

GREEN

I *am* ME. I *am* GREEN

"I am the GARDENER"

I am …
Balanced.
Practical.
Ordered.

GREEN people are the
spectrum's harmonious ones.
Great friends of Nature!

IF YOUR LIFE PATH COLOUR IS GREEN

Dear GREEN, you are the one who encourages us to pause and take a breath, to come back to centre and rebalance. You know and understand that everything has its own 'right' time, and that nothing can be forced or hurried. You teach us when to let go and when to move forward. You bring harmony to all around you and remind us to find or create space in life.

If your Life Path Colour is GREEN, home is important to you. You will strive for balance and harmony in your environment. You need a place to escape the world when you need to.

You have a select and trusted inner circle who you share deep conversations with. This is Green's way of making sense of the world and as a sacred space for self-understanding and healing.

When problems arise, you find comfort in green and natural surroundings. Like Mother Nature, who follows a pattern of seasons, Green people like order and structure. Therefore, a sudden change of plan may be difficult for you to navigate.

Do remember that life is an ever-expanding spiral with no beginning or end. The only thing guaranteed in life is change!

If you are Green, you are practical in all you do. Perhaps working with your hands is something you enjoy? And you like seeing tasks through, even if they are mundane. When the going gets tough, you will always get the job done!

You have a flair for creating harmony from disharmony, and a balanced lifestyle is your ideal. If balance is lacking in life, it will affect you deeply. Your instinct is to restore it at all costs.

People on a GREEN Life Path are dependable and steadfast. They are loving people to be with.

Colour Your World GREEN

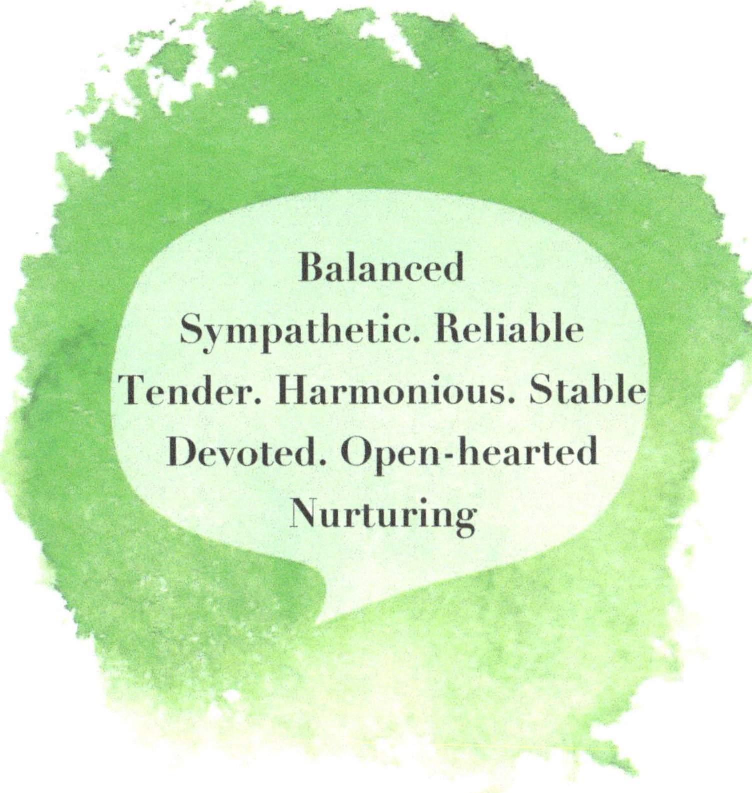

Choose a GREEN word that resonates.
Use it in this AFFIRMATION

"I am ...."

THE LIFE PATH NUMBER

FIVE

IS LIFE PATH COLOUR

BLUE

I *am* ME. I *am* BLUE

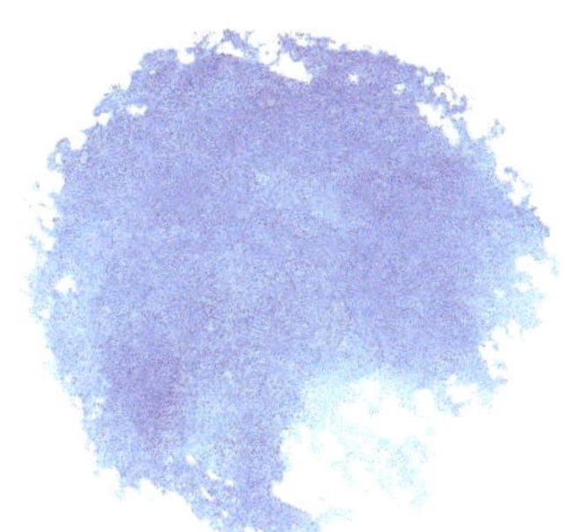

"I am the STORYTELLER"

I am …
    Honest.
    Trusting.
    Communicative.

BLUE people are the
dreamers of the spectrum.
This is a creative Life Path!

IF YOUR LIFE PATH COLOUR IS BLUE

Dear BLUE, you are a natural storyteller with a flair for words, both spoken or written. You have a wonderful way of making people feel at ease and are always willing to lend an ear when someone has a problem or asks for your help.

You are able to listen and then distill the right words in the kindest possible way. This is in order to best serve who you are talking to. People really shouldn't ask if they don't want an honest answer from you. For those who do ask, know that you will always be a kind, trustworthy and loyal confidante.

You are truthful and honest and expect others to be in return. There are no 'grey' areas in this, as far as you are concerned!

Your ability to communicate also extends far beyond speaking or writing. You may also find your voice through art, dance or music. In fact, you communicate through any medium which allows you to speak your own truth.

If your Life Path Colour is BLUE, then your life is one of tranquility and peace, daydreams and adventure. If the idea of adventure and daydreams seems almost paradoxical, this is how you turn ideas into reality. How often have you been told to stop living in the clouds and keep your feet on the ground? But who hasn't, at some point in their life, laid back gazing into the great blue yonder contemplating a different life. Blue, you help remind us to keep things simple and to find the quiet times in life. And perhaps, to daydream a little.

Music and sound are important in your life. But it must be the right piece of music and at the right pitch. If not, your whole system may become irritated, leaving you feeling stressed.

People on a BLUE Life Path have a caring and creative life. Enjoy all that it has to offer!

Colour Your World BLUE

Choose a BLUE *word that resonates.*
Use it in this AFFIRMATION

"I am ...."

THE LIFE PATH NUMBER

SIX

IS LIFE PATH COLOUR

INDIGO

I *am* ME. I *am* INDIGO

"I am the MAGICIAN"

I am …
      Intuitive.
      Reflective.
      Stable.

INDIGO people are the
'seers' of the spectrum.
A special kind of Life Path!

IF YOUR LIFE PATH COLOUR IS INDIGO

Dear INDIGO, you are quite simply, magical! You have an incredible imagination which takes you to places that most of us only dream of. And talking of dreams, whether they are night-time or daytime, epic they certainly are. Your dreams weave storylines of colour and intrigue. No one, except those closest to you would ever know that, would they, Indigo?

You often don't say or share too much but you are the one who sees it all. You have the ability to perceive how and why people act as they do. When all that others see is chaos and disorder, you help us to see the bigger picture and to find order in the grand design of things.

If your Life Path Colour is INDIGO, then you remind us that anything is possible - all we have to do is imagine. After all, everything you see around you started once-upon-a-time in someone's imagination.

You give the appearance of being solid and stable, even if behind the scenes, there is a lot going on for you. You have a psychic or sixth sense ability, but at times you may feel fearful of this gift. Just allow your instinct and your intuition to develop. Trust that it will never let you down.

Indigo people are full of love and understanding. This may not always be obvious because it runs from deep within you. Others will seek your advice and guidance because you see the potential and the possibilities of who they could become.

With all this advice, make sure you give yourself enough time and space to grow in order to fulfil your own potential!

People on an INDIGO Life Path have a special kind of life. Living it to its fullest will reveal miracles, big and small!

Colour Your World INDIGO

Choose an INDIGO *word that resonates.*
Use *it in this* AFFIRMATION

"I *am* ...."

THE LIFE PATH NUMBER

SEVEN

IS LIFE PATH COLOUR

VIOLET

I *am* ME. I *am* VIOLET

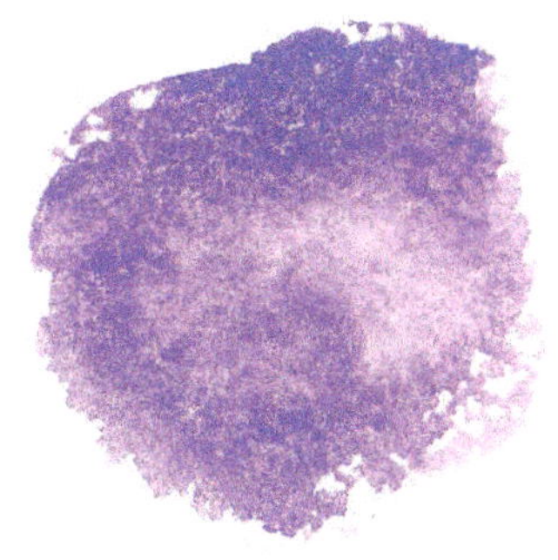

"I am the SOVEREIGN"

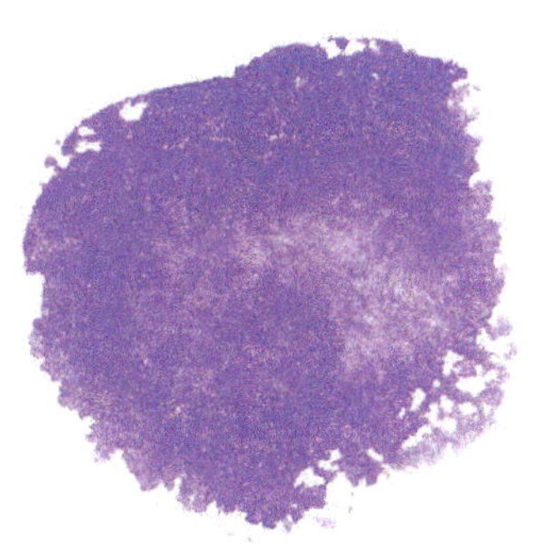

I am …
 Inspiring.
 Confident.
 Creative.

VIOLET people are the leaders of the spectrum. They are one of a kind!

IF YOUR LIFE PATH COLOUR IS VIOLET

Dear VIOLET, how do we honour your royal and majestic presence? Maybe a more pertinent question is, how do you honour yourself in the role you have chosen to play? Your view of the world is far and wide. You ask yourself, why start a small home business when you can start a global empire?

You enter a room with confidence, not in an arrogant or self-important way, but in way that reflects the importance of your role as a leader. Never a follower. You inspire us with your visions of the future. You command attention with elegance, grace and poise. Violet, you remind us that we are born with innate potential to be someone great in the world - even greater than we think we can be.

If your Life Path Colour is VIOLET, then you have probably felt different at some time in your life. In whatever way you may interpreted this feeling, it is positive and a part of being under the influence of Violet. And if you hadn't worked it out already, being Violet makes you stand out from the rest!

Violet people are strong in their beliefs and believe with a passion. You can see what needs changing in this world and how to make a 'Heaven on Earth' for everyone.

You surround yourself with beautiful things, knowing that beauty is not just skin-deep. Violet is the colour of design and opulence and your need to express artistic desires is strong.

With a vivid imagination, a career in the creative world might be just the thing for you. Explore this to your heart's delight!

People on a VIOLET Life Path are like determined and delicate flowers. With guidance and support, you will flourish and grow magnificently.

Colour Your World VIOLET

Choose a VIOLET word that resonates.
Use it in this AFFIRMATION

"I am ...."

THE LIFE PATH NUMBER

EIGHT

IS LIFE PATH COLOUR

ROSE

I *am* ME. I *am* ROSE

"I am the LOVER"

I am …
Loving.
Friendly.
Selfless.

ROSE people are the
guides of the spectrum.
They connect with the world!

IF YOUR LIFE PATH COLOUR IS ROSE

Dear ROSE, you are a Citizen of the World. Your purpose in life is to embrace everyone. This means doing things together and making every effort to unite the world through love. You were given an extra amount of love in order to share its true meaning with all.

Rose people are travellers, crossing countries and continents through work or their social connections. You believe that the world and beyond is one, and that everything is connected.

You bring us all together, reminding us that love unites us. You will never leave anyone behind and are always encouraging us to go further than we think we are capable of. Your passion for a better world is positively contagious.

If your Life Path Colour is ROSE, you are a guide who offers support, advice and comfort. These selfless actions behind the scenes mean letting others take centre stage.

Of course, you are loving to all around you, but remember that you, too, need love and care. Being so concerned for the welfare of those around you, it is natural to ignore things closer to home. But please don't do this, because it might lead you to feel isolated and even lonely.

Be aware of the impact of stress because putting up with too much may see your tolerance fade and your temper show. This may manifest in back issues or bumps and bruises.

Rose people are great organisers, so putting you in charge of a social or business event is a great idea!

People on a ROSE Life Path have a surprisingly natural and harmonious relationship with money. Use it with love.

Colour *Your* World ROSE

Choose a ROSE *word that resonates.*
Use *it in this* AFFIRMATION

"I *am* ...."

THE LIFE PATH NUMBER

NINE

IS LIFE PATH COLOUR

GOLD

I *am* ME. I *am* GOLD

"I am the SAGE"

I am …
Wise.
Discerning.
Thoughtful.

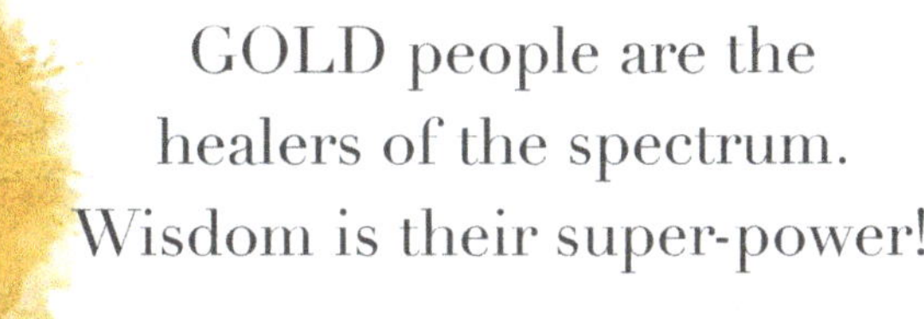

GOLD people are the
healers of the spectrum.
Wisdom is their super-power!

IF YOUR LIFE PATH COLOUR IS GOLD

Dear GOLD, you are timeless, wise and discerning. These are the gifts you bring to the world. You help us learn from the past so we may take this wisdom forward and use it today.

You are timeless as much as you are ageless, being able to sit comfortably and equally amongst the wise elders as you are rolling around on the floor playing with the youngest.

You were born wise. Even from an early age, people around you would tell you their worries. At times, it might have felt like the weight of the world was on your own shoulders!

You have an inner stillness radiating to those around you, inviting them to open up to you and share their stories. You listen without judgement and understand that we all have a past, and equally that everyone has the ability to heal.

If your Life Path Colour is GOLD, then you are also a natural teacher. Even if this is not your profession, you will often find yourself passing on information in one way or another.

You achieve a lot on your life journey and have many talents. However, it may take time to believe in what you can offer.

Yes, you are emotional and you do need to express your feelings. In not expressing them, you may develop issues with low self-esteem. And physically, problems such as aching joints or a weakness of the immune system may arise.

Because you give so much of yourself, time to recharge your energy is important. Having beauty, and especially comfort in your surroundings, will recharge your spirit.

People on a GOLD Life Path are natural healers and teachers. Sharing your healing wisdom with the world is your gift.

Colour Your World GOLD

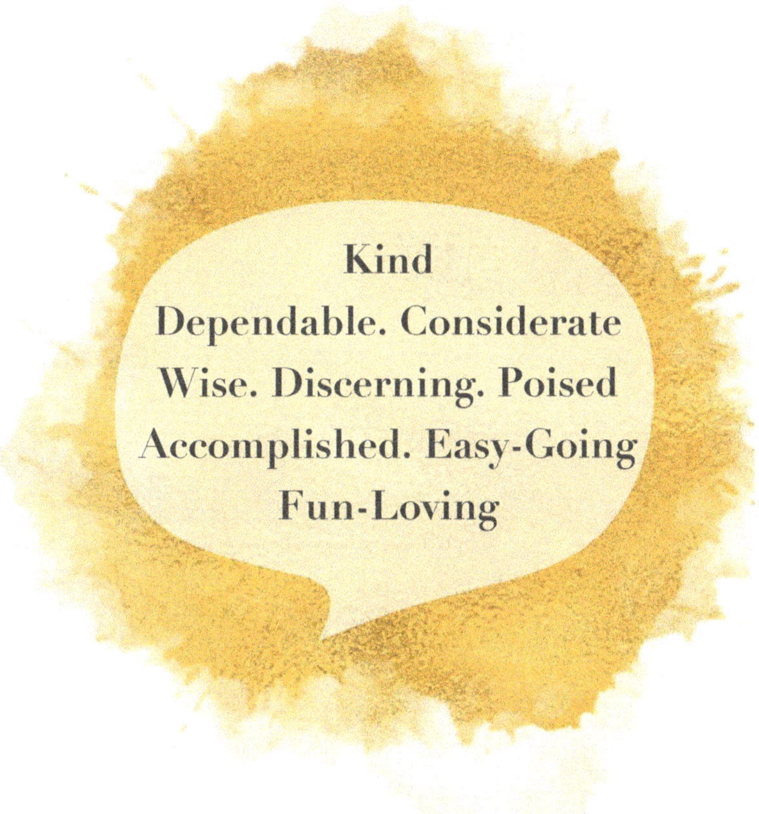

Choose a GOLD word that resonates.
Use it in this AFFIRMATION

"I am ...."

UNLOCKING YOUR COLOUR POTENTIAL

While you can look at, and imagine your colour, there's nothing quite like *becoming* or *being* your Life Path Colour. This means taking intentional action to amplify and strengthen the characteristics symbolised by your own colour.

Each suggestion that follows has been specifically designed, tried and tested to enhance an embodied connection with your colour. Remember that everything you see in your Life Path Colour is, in some way, YOU being mirrored back to you.

Think of your Life Path Colour as a best friend. The kind of friend who knows absolutely everything about you. No matter how many times we feel like we don't belong because we don't have the right shape or the right look; or feel unworthy of the good things in life, this colourful best friend is there for you. Always offering support, always reminding you of how uniquely special you are. This friend knows everything about you, now it is your turn to learn everything about them.

BECOMING YOUR LIFE PATH COLOUR

Choosing your own version of your Life Path Colour is an important first step in *becoming* your colour. It helps you to grow into your colour and get to know it personally. So, choose the shade or tone that appeals to you most.

Finding your special shade of your colour is more about choosing the one which gives you the feeling - "Yes, this is me!" Over time, it may change to a different shade or tone and that's fine. For now, though, just choose one. This is a system that has no 'one colour fits all' approach.

Always keep in mind that you are *never lacking* in your colour. It's just that we all need to let more of our true colour shine out into the world.

Life Path Colours

Follow Your Colour Path

Becoming Red

Feeling stuck or not living as you like doesn't feel good for Reds. You feel your "stuck-ness" physically and that's not good for anyone. Try getting out and taking some action. You may not feel like it but going on an intentional walk - setting an intention for what you want to achieve - and while out walking notice all the signs that Mother Nature gives to you about your intention. When you get home draw or write about the signs and then take some action on the next step.

Becoming Orange

Do you look at your life and only see what you lack? Maybe you see a lack in material things, or perhaps it's a lack of abundance, or a significant other. Whatever it is, if you seem to be in 'lack', the remedy is a big dose of orange. Take some time for yourself and look for the positives you do have in your life. What makes you laugh out loud? If it's a film you've seen many times before watch it again. Cook yourself your favourite meal to remind yourself how special you are. Or invite your 'bestie' for some 'good-time reminiscing'.

Becoming Yellow

Are you a slave to your 101 lists which you have on the go all at the same time? Are you never able to switch off from mental chatter? If this is you, please take a breath. Then take yourself to the store or library for a book about someone who succeeded beyond the odds, someone who took risks and broke free of the "should do's and should be's". You can also create mind-maps to give your mind something positive to focus on. Then watch the clouds of doubt and negative thinking give way to the sunshine yellow rays of hope.

Becoming Green

If time seems to be running away from you and you are feeling overwhelmed with deadlines, then it's time for some Green action. You could start by clearing the clutter. You'll be amazed at how doing this one simple thing can help re-align you with your natural heart-time rhythm. If that doesn't feel like you, then take up mindful breathing and long walks in nature. This can be in the countryside or a suburban park. The important thing is returning to the balance of heartfelt living, following your heart and watching life blossom.

Becoming Blue

Whether it's talking too much and not actually saying anything at all, or realising later what you really wanted to say, then some blue time is what you need. If you talk about what you are going to do but it never quite happens then a bit more blue will help bring your plans into reality. Finding music that calms you or fills you with passion will help you to speak about your hopes for the future. Surrounding yourself with trusting friends who encourage and support you will help you take action towards your dreams.

Becoming Indigo

Are you often lost in thought in your own 'other world' where everything is calm and peaceful allowing you to see clearly? Or is your 'other world' filled with chaos and fears? A chaotic inner world is often part of a deeper creative process, which is why keeping a dream journal and letting your dreams guide you will help you see the way forward to bring the inside outside. Finding a dream group or even exploring lucid dreaming will assist you and help you live the life of your dreams.

Becoming Violet

If you're stuck in routine or doing something that doesn't spark your creative talents, life's hopes and dreams can feel a long way away. What's your BIG vision for the world, what is the one BIG thing you would love to do, yet it scares you as much as it excites you? Once you give yourself permission to acknowledge your 'world player' status, you can start creating plans and drawing out your vision. As you do, notice how the world starts to conspire with you in your vision of making the world a better place. It does so because of your BIG thinking, it does so even if you try to shy away and play small.

Becoming Rose

Like our Red friends, being stuck or having nothing to do is not good for you. It's also not good for anyone else around you! Why not invite some friends for dinner or throw a party to celebrate the joy of sharing and being together with the people you love. Write down all the people and things you love, from that who or what needs more of your attention? Maybe there's someone you are always meaning to meet-up with or a cause you are passionate about but never get round to joining. Act, meet up, join. You'll love it!

Becoming Gold

If all you seem to do is take care of other people instead of yourself, then it's time for some gold therapy! The first part of becoming gold is to remember that it is OK to say NO and not feel guilty about it! The second part is to remind yourself you are worthy of all the good things in life as much as anyone else is. Life doesn't have to be about hardships and struggle to prove you are worthy and deserve happiness. Write or paint the affirmation "I am enough" and/or "I'm allowed to" and feel the golden wisdom of life embrace and nourish you.

" THE JOURNEY THROUGH
THE RAINBOW IS WORTH
ITS WEIGHT IN GOLD "

MARK WENTWORTH

USING COLOUR AFFIRMATIONS

Creating a personalised Colour Affirmation is a potent way of combining the energy of your Life Path Colour with the vibrant power of a personalised statement.

An affirmation is a positive statement to yourself. It can affect and change your mindset, and your way of thinking. Use the power of your colour to choose an affirmation that truly resonates with you - and how you want to feel.

Using your chosen specific shade or tone of colour in your affirmation will make it more a part of YOU as you include it more and more in your life.

In the individual Life Path Colour section of this book, there is a list of words to describe each colour. When you read through them, some will resonate with you more than others. Choose one word that resonates the most; a word that you want to feel like. A word that, perhaps, represents a state of being that you would like to become.

Visualise your own colour as you repeat your own affirmation. Feel the colour. Feel the intention and the power of the word that you have chosen. If visualising is not your thing, then how about drawing or painting it, or creating it digitally.

"AN AFFIRMATION OPENS THE DOOR.
IT'S A BEGINNING POINT ON THE PATH TO CHANGE."

LOUISE HAY

MORE WAYS TO COLOUR YOUR WORLD

Other ways we have found that help to continue the fostering and forging process of this deeply personal colour relationship are:

Keeping a Colour Journal. This is a fun way to start building a relationship with your colour. Start a conversation with your colour. What do you want to say to it? What will it reply? If words aren't your thing, you might journal through collage or even drawing. And on days when life doesn't feel so good, it acts as a lovely reminder of who we really are.

Breathing in your colour. Imagine filling yourself up from the inside-out, letting the special shade of your colour soak into the depths of your being. It's never that we need more of our colour. We just need to let more of it out ... every day.

Drinking your colour. You can do this by solarising water. Use a piece of material of your colour (cotton or silk is ideal) to cover a glass bottle or container filled with water. As long as light can pass through the fabric and using glass is important. Place it in the sun either outside or on a window ledge and leave for a minimum of 3-4 hours. It should be longer if it's a cloudy day. Your 'coloured water' is ready to drink or sip.

Make drinking your colour a daily ritual and take note of how you feel. You might think of it as taking multi-vitamins for the Soul! Try making a different colour and taste the difference. You may be surprised at how differently they taste.

These simple actions tell the Universe that we are saying YES to life. With your Life Path Colour by your side let the magic of life begin. Let the authentic YOU blossom into being.

Here we are, at the end …

We've travelled through this nine-colour rainbow together. Importantly, we've learnt which part of the light spectrum is uniquely ours. And you've discovered how to make your own unique Life Path Colour more visible through ways of being in your day to day life.

For more than thirty-years, we have found these simple steps have brought about profound life-enhancing changes for thousands of people around the world. Even after all this time, the Life Path Colours continue to surprise and delight us in the personal way they reveal themselves to each person. Always unique, always relevant.

Our hope and wish is that as you act upon what you have learnt here, the more happiness and contentment will be revealed to you in your everyday living. Along with the realisation that who you are and what you have to share with the world is totally and fully enough. Just like your chosen shade or tone of colour, YOU are unique,

And on those days when you feel as though your sun doesn't shine, we hope you will remember that your colour is always there for you. It will support you and remind you that just like on a cloudy day, the sun is always there. Still shining brightly.

Journey well, oh, Colour Traveller.

Mark and Amanda

June 2024

ABOUT THE AUTHORS

Amanda Hoffmann has been a teacher of English language and academic studies in colleges and universities, both overseas and in Australia. Since retiring from teaching she has become a continuing student of life. While Amanda has been connected to the world of light and colour for many years as an editor and content creator, this book is a first step into a new role as creator and writer in this subject area. With intentions to spread information and inspiration about colour more widely, she plans to take further steps along this path.

For more information and to contact Amanda:
www.amandajhoffmann.com
Instagram: @a_soultree_journey

Global Colour Ambassador Mark Wentworth has been studying and working with the transformational power of Life Path Colours for nearly forty years. During this time, he created and developed Colour PsychoDynamics®, a three-phase personal growth and mentoring model. Mark works with individuals, teams and businesses using the archetypal language of colour, dreams, drama, film and story as a way of exploring potential, creative projects, new business, stuck points, team building and wellbeing. He travels around the world teaching and sharing his love of colour.

For more information on training and workshops with Mark:
www.colourforlife.com
Instagram: @iamcolourforlife